African Pianism

Twelve Pedagogical Pieces

J. H. Kwabena Nketia

Afram Publications (Ghana) Limited

Published for
International Centre of African Music and Dance

Published by:
Afram Publications (Ghana) Ltd
P.O. Box M18
Accra, Ghana

Tel: +233 302 412 561, +233 244 314 103
            Kumasi: +233 501 266 698
E-mail: sales@aframpubghana.com
            publishing@aframpubghana.com
Website: www.aframpubghana.com

First Published 1994

ISBN: 978 9964 70 147 5
        9964 70 147 0

PREFACE

"**African Pianism** refers to a style of piano music which derives its characteristic idiom from the procedures of African percussion music as exemplified in bell patterns, drumming, xylophone and mbira music. It may use simple or extended rhythmic motifs or the lyricism of traditional songs and even those of African popular music as the basis of its rhythmic phrases. It is open ended as far as the use of tonal materials is concerned except that it may draw on the modal and cadential characteristics of traditional music.

Its harmonic idiom may be tonal, atonal, consonant or dissonant in whole or in part, depending on the preferences of the composer, the mood or impressions he wishes to create or how he chooses to reinforce, heighten or soften the jaggedness of successive percussive attacks. In this respect the African composer does not have to tie himself down to any particular school of writing if his primary aim is to explore the potential of African rhythmic and tonal usages."

Although I have felt the need for this kind of material even in the 1950's, most of the Twelve Pedagogical Pieces in this volume were written when the school of Performing Arts at the University of Ghana was established in the 1960's in order to give the African piano student being nurtured on simplified and original versions of Western piano repertoire something with African rhythmic and tonal flavour that may enrich his experience, shapes his orientation, sense of timing and coordination of rhythmic and tonal events.

As the titles of the pieces indicate, I have used a variety of traditional and popular sources as the basis of the compositions. Each source establishes a framework of rhythmic and tonal configuration from which a few idiomatic derivatives are made and used in the inner and outer structures of the piece in such a way as to create a perpetual feeling of propulsive motion. Each piece is sustained by a particular quality of motion created in this manner.

As in traditional African practice each piece can be repeated once or twice except where a definite closure is indicated by a retard. The pianist can also select a number of them and play them as a suite. A few of them such as the Volta Fantasy and Meditation can stand on their own as concert pieces and have been presented in that manner by both African and Western pianist. It is my hope, therefore, that some of the pedagogical pieces will be of general interest.

J. H. Kwabena Nketia

PLAY TIME

(c. 1957)

1

Fine

mf

D.C.

OWORA

(c. 1965)

4

5

AT THE CROSS ROADS

(c. 1961)

RAYS OF HOPE

(After Kaakaiku)

(c. 1963)

9

LIBATION

(After E. K. Nyame)

(c. 1975)

10

11

MEDITATION

(c. 1961)

15

16

DAGARTI WORK SONG

(1967)

19

BUILSA WORK SONG

(c. 1948)

VOLTA FANTASY

(c. 1967)

24

25

89

94

99

104

108

DAGOMBA

(c. 1946)

rit. 2nd time

ABSENT FRIENDS

(c.1969)

AKPALU

(c. 1970)

34

Printed in the United States
By Bookmasters